Monster Zero

Jay Snodgrass

Winner of the
2002 Second Annual Elixir Press Poetry Awards

ELIXIR PRESS

Monster Zero

ISBN: 0-9709342-6-2

Cover Design: Collin Hummel
Layout Design: R. F. Marsocci

Elixir Press
P. O. Box 18010
Minneapolis, MN 55418
www.elixirpress.com
info@elixirpress.com

Acknowledgments

Grateful acknowledgment is made to the following publications in which some of these poems have appeared:

The Chiron Review: "Godzilla Sits Down to Watch Cable" and "Godzilla's Eastward Movement"

Firebush: "News Report"

Slipstream: "Little Things"

Shenandoah: "Godzilla Dreamed of a Man Planting Rice"

I would like to thank Denise Duhamel and Campbell McGrath, the faculty at Florida International University, Clay Blancett, Mary Boyes, George Tucker, William Whitehurst, Terri Carrion, Laura Valeri, Bill and Tom Snodgrass, William Tester, Laura Browder, and Tom DeHaven for their support and unerring faith. I would like to thank Rita, Mary Ann, Hugo, and Brandt for their criticism. "Godzilla Dreamed of a Man Planting Rice" is dedicated to the memory of Larry Levis, without whom none of this would have occurred. I would also like to thank Mitch, Hana, and especially Kristine for their patience and inspiration.

For Kristine

and
For my Mother and Father

Contents

Planet Zero

Planet Negative One

Godzilla,
You were born in the year of the universal explosion.
Millions of oceans were swept out to sea.

We share futility like a coat,
Something to wear when others are watching.

We will meet under fallen leaves.
They become ash
As the sun goes south
For vacation.

Little Things

In Tokyo you can buy a miniature, idealized Godzilla
Rounded out in the shape of a baby.
A fun thing from something terribly fun,
Or terrible, and so made for children—
Anything really that large and destructive
Could only be understood by the molding hands of a child,
The mind of a child's finger
Circling around the image of itself as destroyer.
The toy is egg-shaped and sometimes comes
In the little plastic egg containers dispensed
From the machines you put a coin in and turn the gear.
A little plastic ball drops into your hand
As though by an act of contrivance the machine
Had given birth, for your fingers, to your hand,
The fingers cupped together in a valley,
A valley being defined as the construction of things that
Cannot hold water. In the same way
The bombardier pilot for the *Enola Gay*
Wets himself as the bomb bay doors open up
And the guidance machine takes over for the thirty seconds
Before delivery, wrenching the knobs from his fingers
To assume a life of its own.
A life in which things are born
To do terrible things in terrible shapes.
The small metal door of the gumdrop machine,
Sending out happy little plastic monsters
Into the fingers of the world
Making everything grow small
Until every part of the world is just a smaller part
Of calamity, every human eye a number in the catalogue
Of the giant spinning atrocity.

Godzilla Romances Tokyo

I know the way the bay grows dark
When the water shawls over like a mirror,
Its smooth floor where

I keep a sunken battle ship,
The only marker before you, Tokyo,
The submerged curve of you, rises up.

At night, when you turn on your face
And look at yourself in the bay's mirror,
The bars of light neon ripple

And the single room lights
Left on in the high-rises sparkle
Like a fifty yen coin.

The coin has chrysanthemums
On one side circling
Around and around a hole.

Inside that silver is a darkness you
Could put a string through
And tie around your neck

As a reminder, a keepsake.
Sometimes I lean over your
Shoulder to see what you are

Looking at. I wink one eye
At a single glinting light and guess
If that's the one you are looking at.

Tonight I won't disturb
Your strange privacy.
The ocean itself disturbs your reflection.

But I'll let you in on a secret:
It's no accident that the light,
Incandescent, is rippled like scales.

In Tokyo, Certain Types of Matter Emit Energy Along the Contours of the Road

An old man rides a bicycle between the white line
And the edge of broken asphalt stones,
He hunches into the wind, into the silencing
Roar of a landing C-5A Galaxy, the largest
Airplane used by the American military.
By now the effects of an artificially decomposed
Nucleus have been felt, the oceans are moving,
Everything is crumbling, the stones beneath the wheels
Careen off one another into the road and into the grass.
The old man is wearing a brown driving hat,
His bicycle is blue, the tires are black.
He fenders his way towards me out of history,
He has apples in his basket. The mountains
Are cold in the cloudless distance,
They give shape to the emptiness, which is worse
Than not knowing that there is no edge.

Godzilla Dreamed of a Man Planting Rice

Who rose, all day bent double, to see
The flash of the Hiroshima bomb.
All day the drone of decoy bombers
Set fire to the cities, while he went on

Planting rice. I believe it was a moment
For which the man felt nothing, his feet
Wet, his back bent permanently
From bending, pushing seedlings
Into mud through the reflection of his

Face framed by the sky, green in the patty
The clouds still white, still passing
Above him, or below him. It didn't matter.
It was just a flash and a sudden wind to him.
He could hear the sound of singing in the distance.

I don't know much about madness
But that it lives in the body like a harp string,
Beside the heart, makes it painful to move.
That bowing your body towards madness
Gives slack to it, but also

Changes the note. Maybe I have dreamed
Of a dead man, who I have buried
Inside me so that I can listen until
I hear the sound of a distant note
Through the dead branches of my skull.

I wonder if it is possible
To give music to the dead, to watch over them
With statue eyes, until they are finished
With their work.

After Larry Levis

6

Godzilla Wanted to Move to the City

Away from his mother the ocean,
In order to feel the culture by immersion.

So he packed his plastic skin
And went for an interview
With a doll maker who made doll

Clothes for all the simple children
And their careless mothers.
He wanted to feel the culture by immersion,

Not the inversion he was used to,
Eating it all up, internalizing
His anger and burning people alive.

Godzilla wanted to move to the city,
To be faceless riding the subway
Or unknown at a late night movie,

He wanted to feel the culture by immersion
Not the way it was when
Everyone worshipped you as destroyer.

Godzilla moved to the city
Where he made dresses for dolls
That children might burn

As they grew up, as children
Like to burn the artifices of culture,
As a means of expression, an immersion.

Three Thousand Feet Under Bikini Atoll

Godzilla, is that my name?
It sounds so beautiful,
Like a whisper the clouds empty
Themselves in.

If I look up through the water toward the sky
I can read my face there.
Does it matter that I don't feel the spines
Like a ridge of mountains down my back?

The rush hour train couldn't hold me.
I tried to ride it like a skate downtown,
Trying to beat King Ghidera to the Diet Building,
Always empty by the time we got there.

The American fire bombing of Tokyo
Took the breath from the city,
I took the formal robes out of Japanese government.
I knew it wouldn't make sense, small mouths
Stretching into esthetic Os, the tiny eyes set close.

I enjoy salons, powders, perfumes.
I want red cheeks like a noble woman,
A blush of courage or a secret moment.
Instead I have marble green in my eyes
And a tongue of perfect fire.

In front of the mirror, the face I have inherited
From old meat and fermenting skin,
Jurassic passions and medieval sins
Falls inward into me, beneath the water,
A sudden implosion of all elements,
A body linked to a chain of ancestors
Resembling suns growing dark on themselves.

This is how I lose the war with my face.

Godzilla Remembers Himself
as an Angel of Mercy

At first I was an angel, uncontrollable,
Unaccountable, as the stars.

Before, when I was an angel,
When the patterns of leaves moved
Like pouring water,
Before the patterns of snakes,
There was grace, spreading itself over everything like a veil.

That was me, before, when I was an angel.
That was everything, heaven was clear
Like an empty memory.

And then I was gone,
Right after Nietzche said god was dead,
I was gone for a long time.
Then I came back
With a face I didn't recognize.
It was like I'd failed at something.

And then I came back in parts,
Wave after wave of hazy open spaces
Like a plain, wide open with horses running,

Part window, part glass,
Part flowing thing, like ocean, mother
And annihilator,

Part disease, part plague, part toad
And part crocodile, part
Eater part eaten, like an open door,

Part table linen, part undergarment
Tangled, part untangled like a
Spider web, part fly,

Part tender flesh, part slaughter house,
Part of everything held back,
Part watching, part open mouth.

Godzilla Leafs Through
a Crate & Barrel Catalogue

Kitchen table, you are missing from my life.

In fact, you are never there for me
When I tread barefoot
Into the house needing only
A place to sit and a shelf to
Rest my arm on as I watch
The road slip away
Through the window

While the blanket of evolution ($99.99)
Draws itself over the moon.

Godzilla *vs.* Iguanadon

Beneath the light of neon crosses sizzling
Old marriage vows out into the night,
A woman dressed barely in her skin
Waits for a glitter-red El Camino.

She repeats the wedding vows
The moon has written on the sidewalk's
Thousand paving stones.

She reaches for the door handle
And glides away in the serpent-backed
Machine, feeling as though
She's just been eaten.

She is removed into the supple
Night on the hiss of black tires
As dark fingers girdle
Her knees like fearful claws.

Godzilla in Drag

I wish I had worn that dress, the red one, so bright
against my green skin, it makes me feel like a Hawaiian princess.
I wanted so bad for people to notice me, to get out
     from under their desks
and upturned cars, that I actually thought of offering them sex.
But I never did because I never got the chance. No one wanted me
to come, let alone come near them. So I go to this night club,
The Bomb Crater, and whenever I caught a guy looking
at me I'd draw my amphibious lids up so my eyes go
from green to gray. I thought it was as good a signal as any,
the way people go scurrying when they feel
     the vibrations of my feet
like a Richter scale. But all the men turned away, it was
     looking like a total loss.
When in walks this three-headed guy, big as a building
     and full of himself,
you can just tell. Sure, he notices me right away and saunters over,
one head looking at me the whole time, the other two
     checking out other girls.
I didn't want him to think I was desperate, so when he lurched
up beside me, leaned back on his long tail and said
I just came in from Planet X and I'm looking to stir up some trouble,
I knew what he wanted. But I only wanted him to want me
so I said I had all the trouble he could handle. What can I say,
I was horny. He said his name was Ghidera,
and he laughed and we went out into the night trampling cars
and food vendors, soba carts and cigarette machines.
Everything seemed to come together under our feet,
a recombination of things. Everything wrong felt right.
I squashed a man buying school girl's underpants
     from a vending machine,
and a Moped courier bringing defense plans to the parliament.
I would have crushed them all if Ghidera asked me to, his whole
body smooth like a crocodile in water.
I felt like rubber next to him, self conscious of my giggling. I tried
to tighten myself around an official motorcade, but the cars
     burst into flame

when I touched them. He laughed at that too. I tried to be
     seductive, dribbling
burning gasoline down his chest. He grabbed me and kissed
     me with one
head and bit me with another. I should have known his third head
was looking around for another girl all the while.
I suggested we go back to my place which was quiet and several
hundred feet underwater. But he didn't want to, said he
     had to get across
town before someone figured to bring in tanks. I was as seductive
as I could be but he said he was controlled by the aliens on Planet X
and that if he didn't get at least halfway through Tokyo by dawn
they were going to fry his brains out with radiation. So I
turned a full blast of my own radiation breath on him,
called him a cheat and a liar and scorched his most sensitive head
black. Apparently he liked the rough stuff.
He picked me up and flew me into the crater on top of Mt. Fuji
where we rolled around on top of a ski lodge. He was
     done in seconds
but I understood. It was when he got up and pretended that he still
had to destroy the city when I really got mad. I charred him
     up again
and burned him back down to the city. He cried but I felt strong
and pretty and I wanted him to know that Earth
was a burning place too and that no Planet X monster could come
here and trample things and leave me feeling used in a crater.
I stomped on his heads and scorched his tail again
and again, setting fire to most of the city as an afterthought.
People screamed as they burned to death,
when I looked at them I didn't feel sorry, it was what I did too.
As Ghidera flew back to outer space he turned and waved,
one head mouthing thanks. Around me the city burned.
I swam the long swim of shame
back to my radioactive lair.

Godzilla to Tokyo

What if the city falls now
and only dust shuffles in my shoes?
I come to the window, looking out.
Here a row of corn, here a street,
there a row of buses waiting.
The setting sun shines a spider web,
the spider stitches useless circles
around factories in the distance.
If the city falls now
would I remember this?

These little wars of futility,
the silking of a house fly,
its back a lacquered candy,
This spinning round a shell,
soft inside drawn hollow,
the mitered edge of wings connecting
just above a candycane-striped
smokestack in the distance.

And beyond
the rows of houses
and back yard vegetable gardens,
rows of cars left empty on the streets,
power lines a jagged string
of chaos in connection.

I squint my eye to all of this
and wonder how
the spider finishes
its sculpted meal
with a thread
pulled from the sky.
As I wink it becomes a blurry whiteness
twice as big as anything.
I feel the breathing wind
and think what nonsense
it must be to live.

Godzilla Sits Down to Watch Cable

He flips on the remote and begins to thumb through
Five hundred channels of digital cable.
He likes the civilization channel. He hopes to find clues
To his identity there. He moves past the
Channel that's airing his movies. By contract
He is not allowed to watch them, in fact,
By contract, he has no memory of them whatsoever.
He likes that all the movie channels are arranged by theme.
That way he can just go to the Romance Channel
And hug his large pillows. His pillows are red and
Have Chinese characters stenciled on them.
He thinks it is a poem but he can't read what it says.
The tag says they are silk but washable.
Sometimes he cries himself to sleep on the pillows
And has to wash them the next day or they'll melt.
Watching a love story is a way he can have feelings
Without breech of contract.
Today he settles on a western, a mystical experience
He allows himself in secret. He doesn't want to
Be seen as childish, but he likes it when the Hero wins.
He watches for the showdown scene, the high noon,
The explosion of sunlight on a black and white
World. What he imagines every time is that
The gunmen, the good and the bad, will draw
And pull their triggers at the exact same instant,
That their bullets will be vectored into exact trajectories,
Moving at each other with the same velocities,
The good growing negative and the bad growing positive
Until they reach the Zero Point, where everything is nothing,
And they cancel each other out. Godzilla hopes
The world is cut into mathematical light and dark, he imagines
That is the place where he was born.

Godzilla's Eastward Movement

There is nothing east of Japan but Iwo Jima.
Just now, I can sleep again. If I dream,
There is a fire. Brown uniformed soldiers
Crouch around it. They are the only
Human beings left in the Pacific Ocean.
They want to kill me.
They look into the fire for hours,
Or out into the dark ocean.
At night the ocean dissolves,
Only a gentle breathing expresses the
Half-life of decay.
In, out, I am wandering
Through this process
Searching for a hole in the darkness.
The soldiers, mesmerized by fire,
Scoop gobs of darkness from the sky
To polish their guns with.

Planet One

Godzilla,
Born of an eternal sound,
Atoms dissolving across the universe,
Can be heard on special radios
Hissing everywhere.

First Confession

Algebra

The year they showed us the movie *The Day After*,
About surviving a nuclear war, all my expectations
About the future vaporized.
At the junior high I went to on an airbase
In Tokyo they were nice to me
And let me gently slip through the cracks.
I remember the light coming through the windows
Of the school and the sound of airplanes.
One day there was an earthquake and the kid who
Sat next to me in Algebra had a seizure. All I could do
Was stand there pointing at him with one hand, the
Other covering my mouth while the teacher tried
To put his wallet between the kid's teeth. I felt like
I had been let in on a secret everyone else was kept
In the dark about. When I confessed to another
Student that I was afraid of the end of the world,
He bought me a heavy codeine
Syrup from a chemist downtown and I got lost
In the mountains until I graduated. Later, when I
Drove off in my father's car there was a light
Coming from the fields, the rows and rows
Of tea bushes, it brushed at the mist in the lower
Places until the whole world just shined.
At school I learned that an equation
Is when everything on both sides of the equal sign
Balances. After a while I stopped
Crying about the things I couldn't change.
After a while the fatigue in my heart lifted
So that airplanes didn't sound like
Bombers anymore. Now they speak to me
About their love for light, and when I hear them
I nod, knowing that theirs is a doomed romance.

Second Confession

1.

I called up from the supremacy of myself a tiny
    mystical shadow
In which wings fluttered and I was great, singularly
By being unknown.

One hand on glass, I poke my head out to survey
That sound riding over the walls of stillness.
You can't remember the last time you heard
    Punjab spoken on a cell phone.

Little quasi mysteries, I dole them out to myself
    just by being alive.

Frigate bird, chancellor bird, memories of other
    inhabitants and times
When humans built livable lives on curiosity.
What do we all know about anything that matters?
    When the pennies fall
From other peoples' pockets as they reach for their
    keys in the supermarket parking lot,
I know I will be there to find them.

2.

The itinerant message of suffering,
The bold incalculable resonance of turning
From one slithering awareness to another.

3.

I grew with the light and the light grew through me.

4.

If you think a thought about yourself
And then you think a thought about yourself

Thinking about yourself thinking a thought
About yourself and so on, then

You can't stop seeing yourself through
Someone else's eyes, and ultimately you

Don't know who you are anymore because
You can't remember which of you looking at the other

Yous was the first one. And so the fragments look
Around, looking for the first and they grow

Multiply on themselves until they are a
Giant dinosaur-shape of mind-eyes looking.

This is how we split into fragments.

5.

I am becoming
More obscure as the tires of oblivion drive at me
With a growing hiss that is neither warning or damnation.
You gave me a kiss one night
Just after the rain, the wind came up and dried me a little,
I was wet and that conspired to maintain me.
The things I assumed were shriveling up,
And then the light found me out, showered me with
    a kind of warmth
That was neither light nor heat, but understanding,
Understanding that dominated the need to be fueled
By any feeding. I was not to eat, but to be eaten,
As the flowers ate up the space around them and turned all
Eyes into looking things with no will
But that of pleasure. I am escaping, and inescapable,
These are the dimensions of my
Paradox—give to me all that's required of dying and I will
Assume that it's all mine.
These are my memories, join me at the table and feel yourself
Cringing from the torrent of rain
Breaking up large cliffs outside and everywhere in here.

6.

Don't look at the flowers for the flowers,
Don't pretend that there is any truth to the presumptions
You made when you were getting ready
To reject or except everything there was to believe in:
The gods abounding, the hollowness without them,
There had to be some kind of acceptance
Yearned for, the only thing we all wanted.

7.

I am never hopeless. I can't be.
There is some mechanism that won't let me give up.
It's the same kind of mechanism that drives people off
    building tops.

This is the purpose—to make the mind see not itself as a whole
But as some part of itself.
This is the matter of cohesion.

These are the small dots
we find all over our memories,
the little spaces, the really important ones
we can't remember because we choose
not to and then we wonder what it is we can't remember
and we want it back so we fill in the empty spaces
with good pictures of ourselves
and the course of self mockery
that is our selves is what makes up our lives.
This all sounds rather bleak, I'm sure.

8.

What, whatever, the mix, interminable.
Remember the red blooming hibiscus, there, in the afterglow?
We charged ourselves to be wandering the streets. Don't
    you know how
Everything radiates out from the sun like seeing itself,
Becoming outright; challenging itself like the simple
Undercurrent of the self?

Third Confession

Interrogation

1.

You called me here because I am a curse,
A scourge to mankind,
How are we the same?

Sometimes the light looks just the same
As it did before when I was someone else.
But the birds aren't the same, which means the clouds
Who bred them have different sources,
Different mothers like the sea.

I wake up and I never lived ten thousand miles away
Across the Pacific.

Power lines over the train tracks
Cut the light into time,
The tide into soft beach,
Each swipe sucks my feet as I stand there
Further down
Through sand, through the eroded remnants
Of earth, days wiped away
Until everything is buried

And I remember my brothers burying me in the sand,
My willingness to submit to the experiment,
My fear when I couldn't move anymore
That they would leave me there
A victim of the tide.

When there's no where to look but up
The sky becomes a stranger too,
And if I could wade between the two,
I'd be passing through light
On my way from foreigner to resident.

2.

You are guilty of watching me,
Of seeing my disasters.
You are charged with pulling
The memories of all the dead
Behind you in a wagon.

This means I was born in America
A week before my father left for Vietnam,
November, 1970.
          It's easy being born at the beginning of a decade,
I can always tell how old I am.
While in Vietnam my father never wore a uniform,
He traveled as a journalist surveying the land
Through the mouths of people;
While I goo goo-ed my way through a south Florida
Winter, he had to check the calendar to see what
Month it was.
                    While America was parading its way
Through rice fields in the name of freedom,
My father was watching from distant hilltops
For secondary explosions after B-52 raids.

My eyes had not yet learned to focus.
My father came back and I never knew he was gone.

I suppose my first visions were of the light
Through water on the bottom of a pool; like a drunken
Man coming to I must have thought it celestial.

My father watched a caravan of trucks snake through a valley,
He turned around and was knocked foreword by concussion.
When he looked back it was
As though there had never been any trucks.

When he came back from his tour he took a post in Japan,
My earliest memories are Japanese: stone pagodas

Ponds of dry white stones, blue mountains
Against blue mountains into the distance.

As an adult now, I don't believe I can lay claim to them,
I never learned to speak the language.

How do you plead?

Fourth Confession

Why Godzilla?

Because everyone wants to have his finger on the button.

Because everyone is afraid.

Because the cicadas are deafening
Through the ash grove.

Because everyone wants to be huge
To scare away worry.

Because the Americans dropped two bombs
On Hiroshima and Nagasaki
And my father was in the military
Stationed in Japan
And when I was thirteen he took me to
See the cities forty years afterwards.

Because I can imagine myself at war
Every war.

Because even atoms are made of atoms
And universes are atoms for more universes.

Because I read science fiction as a child.

Because I played war as a child.

Because I didn't understand why
When I was twelve the Japanese held
An anti-nuclear armament rally
And paraded around the base,
I thought they were attacking and
I went to the MPs at the gate
To enlist.

Because there were old plastic
Store displays of Ultraman and Godzilla
Used as scarecrows in a chestnut grove.

Because they were vending machines.
Because I climbed over the barbed wire
To put ten yen coins into them.

Because I hoped they would give me
Some truth, some secret,
Something I always wanted
But never had.

Because I grew up in Japan
But I always wanted to grow
Up in the states.

Because I wanted to grow up in California.
Because that was normal.

Fifth Confession

1. Godzilla My Therapist

Childhood is a wound
The skin grows over until
Buried somewhere deep inside
You can still feel the bump
You once were.

Yokota Air Base—
My friend Jose and I steal a pack of my mother's
Benson & Hedges and sneak into
The old barracks which are about to be demolished.
We open the window onto the setting sun
And open the door for air flow, so no one can
Smell the smoke, even though no one would
Be coming. We leave foot prints in the dust.
With a match I'm proud I know how to strike,
I learned from watching my mother,
I light a cigarette and mimic the draw of breath
But I don't know how to inhale.

Jose and I puff and blow feeling the bitterness
Dry our mouths, from the window we can see
Across the fence and into the shop fronts that
Line the outside perimeter road. We think if
Someone out there sees us they'll tell,
We think we're that important. We're less than a mile
From the flight line, a plane roars in to land,
The glass shakes and we think we're being caught.

We smell exhaust from the street,
From our own mouths
But we don't know how to take it in,
To believe it, and then the worst,
We don't know how to put out the cigarette
So we leave it on the window ledge
And run. Outside we can
Still see it smoking and the sky
Has the white cigarette of con tail.

2. Godzilla as Police Sketch Artist

I ride my bike around the back end of the flight line
To get to football practice. There's a light on the road
And a bell that goes off when a plane's coming in
Like a regular railroad crossing. When the plane
Comes in the bell goes off and I ride as fast
As I can before the next plane comes. When I
Pass over the actual runway I look down
At the lines of lights, the directionals and guiders,
Purple flashers and red arrows and giant
Blue chevrons mark the land zones at their points.
I squint at the kaleidoscope and remember the story
Of the cyclists who got caught out there,
One got thrown back in the gravity well,
The other was sucked up into the turbine.

3. Godzilla Splits Me Like an Egg

The bright glare off aluminum buildings
Dazzles as the train clatters away
From the Peace Park towards Hiroshima
Station. Around a curve
The wooden floor and leather straps
Creak as bodies shift from side to side
Like sailors at sea. Through the window
Children run along the sidewalk,
Taxis queue in stands on a street gritty with
The residue of human cargo. A dirty
Rivulet of water left over from a sudden
Rain clogs the gutters. Everything is new
And dirty, everything is covered over
With the skin of asphalt and pavement.
This is Hiroshima and I am thirteen years old.
I look at the new buildings and they
Don't hum with radiation, and the children
Are born normal. I didn't know any of this then.

We'd looked at the museum,
The pictures of devastation, the burning,
Presented as though it were just
A flood or a hurricane.
There was an obelisk bristling with thousands
Of origami cranes, and a giant bell
Ten feet high with a log on a rope
Like a battering ram to ring it,
Resonating down to our molecules.

When I looked at the scale model
Of the city in a round basin like a bath
With a red ball hanging over it, I didn't
Know what I was looking at,
I didn't understand about radiation.

I didn't really know
That the world was round.
I had the concept, I could answer
It right on a test, but I had no
Idea what distance was, how the Earth
Spun away from itself while you watched,
How from everywhere you stood
There were people all over the world
Above and below you, coming at you
And dropping away.

Before I got to Hiroshima
I thought I was innocent,
That I could be blamed for nothing.

Just as we were passing the dome of
The tourism office, the one building they
Left, one of the few left standing,
A domed office building, the girders
Of the dome surviving, a clutch of
Iron fingers around an empty skull,
A drunk old Japanese man got on the train,

Zeroed in on me—the only foreigner—
As though he'd just discovered a curiosity
He'd overlooked. He lurched into me
Holding himself up
With a bony finger against my chest,
And pointed with his other hand at the dome
And said *You did this.*

I didn't know
But when my mind hit that moment
It split into two halves,
Two selves.

4. My Childhood as a Monster

In an alley behind the house where I grew up,
A grove of chestnut trees,
A garrison of vagabond cats,
And a pair of man size plastic
Godzilla-shaped vending machines
Used as scarecrows.

Through the middle, a path of muddy ruts
Banked by soft moss.
At either end a road
Cuts me off from wanting to leave.
Snow patches the ground in shady spots.

The world is crisp and clear.

If I stand still long enough
The cats will approach me.

They begin to believe
I am another monster,
And I become a walnut
In a grove of soft moss.

5. Playing Godzilla

In my childhood movie I remember the bulk of August
Humidity, the heat had a major role. In the field I passed through
On my way to the video arcade, the chestnut trees were extras,
A crowd of arms reaching after me.
The smell of moldy wood was Daryl Hannah
As the android Priss in *Blade Runner*,
A female character played by someone overly talented
At lounging—it's the lounge allure that gives weight
To the smell of humidity-wet compost.
That August heat was a big rubber Godzilla suit
In which there was no one, only the mimicry of motion,
A chest rising and falling with breath. There was
No one on the planet but me and some change I had
In my pocket for the games. Passing through the grove
The spiky seeds of horse chestnuts were
Superman's baby ice pod, the one his father, Jarel,
Played by Marlon Brando, put him in
And sent him off to be Christopher Reeves 3 or 4 times.

I am crash landed in that field. The empty green suit
Comes at me night after night from my memories.
Inside is Gene Hackman chasing me through the subway
In the *French Connection*. Running, I turn into a moldy
Old building which becomes a field and my feet
Cracking branches becomes Rutger Hauer crashing through
A wall in *Blade Runner* and breaking Harrison Ford's fingers
This is for Zora, this is for Priss. And every crack
Is the empty Godzilla suit walking at me in the empty woods.

What happens in this scene is I take off all my clothes
And step into the heat of the Godzilla suit, fill
My lizard pockets with the superman nut shells
Which I use for quarters in video games and I spend
The rest of the film set August of my life playing
Missile Command and Asteroids, wearing
A suit everyone recognizes from the prop department.

6. At the Peace Park Museum

There is a photo of the dome
Just after the explosion.
No people, only the bare head
Of the structure suddenly
Alone against the flatter horizon.

Walking out from the Smithsonian
Museum of Air and Space—where they refused
To house the *Enola Gay* exhibit—
You can see the dome of the Capitol Building.
The Neoclassical columns that make it
Look like a Roman temple do not hold
Anything up, they are purely decorative.
In the photograph
My father took of me across the Reflecting
Pond they are missing altogether—
They were being replaced by new columns
That would fill the gap between
The dome and whatever is supposed to
Hold it up.
The old columns are in the
National Arboretum now
Pretending to be ruins.

Sixth Confession

1.

I didn't know what you looked like.
I had to piece you together from history,
From when I hated god for leaving me alone
In Japan. It was so far away
But I didn't know from what.
I was looking at the concrete
And then I looked up and I was foreign,
I recognized exile.
I cursed god because
The open blue sky was the same one
Shining in the U.S.
I cursed god and you were there,
I cursed god because I didn't know.

2.

I am not the train,
I am not the rail,
I am not the rocks in the gutter,
I am not the hydrangea
Unsettled like hair in the wind,
I am not the reflection in the glass
Or the face looking at my back in the glass,
I am not the sun on the rail,
I am not the shadow crawling down the wall,
I am not the warning—don't look,
Don't look here,
There's nothing to see here.

3.

Where the rails separate at the tie,
The sound of crickets in darkness,
My ears are listening.

I am a boy looking into the world
And hearing nothing. I am using my eyes
To see there's nothing left.

How the sounds on the rail are like the tick of a clock,
How every clock is a time bomb.

4.

All of this in a room
Where you want me to tell you
What I mean by unpronounceable reaching.

Fear?

5.

If I open my eyes
I am amazed. In the brightness
Outside the window my face
Appears to me a canceled message,
A sudden, startling, disconnected tone.

Somewhere in a hotel
A TV is on. A couple
Love each other without
Learning how or what
They look like, their
Clothes are in a heap
On the floor, only
Their legs, mangled
Together let us know
They are in love.

I watch all this
Through the train window,
I think of how many people
Died, how many of them were
Soldiers.

What are a few lives against thousands,
Millions? What is a refugee
With no skin? A vanishing crowd,
Passing concern, History
Showing the darkness of its mouth
Behind sudden teeth.

6.

I don't care about anything
Because of the sound of the sunlight.

The train car is silent like a house
Filled with sunlight in which no one
Is awake yet. I have a toy,
I wonder if anyone is awake
Anywhere in the world.

I click click Godzilla's tail
And the tongue marches into the light
And back into the shadow of mouth.

The sound leaps out to me
From a dream where the winds
Of a strange world clatter
Sand against a steel pipe
In which I am hiding.

Something is coming
For me, which means something
Is coming.

Seventh Confession

Kanji

I used to snort paint pens in biology class,
One finger closing one nostril, one eye squinting,
Again and again as
The girls would write *I love you*
Across their notebooks. I'd sniff so hard
Wanting to feel my way across the trees
Out the third floor window
That made the world seem awkward.

I remember glimpses under steel desks
Of Christine Inoue, half Italian,
Half Japanese. She was the first time
I fell in love. With her fingers pushing
Out shapes from clay in Art class,
The red clay on her wet hands, her
Touching shapes, caressing them
Over and over.

I gave up self destruction
For arts and crafts,
For a half Japanese girl;
Second generation, they say,
Damaged goods.

But what was I?
Learning to write my name
In the letters reserved for foreign words,
Learning to write *I love you* in Kanji,
In gold paint. Where did she go?
Stray freckles on her thigh,
High up under her skirt,
Under the steel desk?

Did she become the light
Tripping between languages like
The day shifting across the tree tops?
Did she become another country?
Adding to the confusion,
Changing colors,
Disappearing beneath the lines
Of a Chinese paint brush.

That year something happened,
I began to lose myself in the print
Of leaf shadow on the ground,
There were words there I couldn't understand—
Pictures and names, undecipherable,
Brushed by the wind.

And then autumn dropped all the leaves,
All the names were swept up by the Kanji for broom,
Swept into bags, endless black bags
Of unwritten names, some forgotten
Some unremembered.

I changed then, growing up,
I remember being in love with clay,
With myself and then another,
Fingers and trees,
And then I forgot it all.

Planet Zero

I have disputed the birthplace of Godzilla.
Let all the world gleam like a sunset
In the eye of another planet.

Godzilla's Two Legs

The right one is fine,
Hopeful about the future,
Leaning a little forward,
Childish and expectant,
Well muscled beneath
Gleaming scales that radiate
Like an oil slick in sunshine;
Claws gleaming with dark light.

The left
Is scarred from the sharp edges
Of refinery tanks
Edged like aluminum cans
All the way down
To the strangely
Human-like heel.
One would think
He'd have elongated
Tarsus like a dog
So he could run faster,
But the heel is a white oval,
Soft as an egg.

Even though it's all scarred up
It's the leg he leans on when
He heaves back to kick open
An apartment building,
Or to dance a little victory
Dance. The left one is the one
On which he exposes himself.

The right leg keeps itself occupied
With calamity, seeking out
Pain to deliver. It is rigid
And alert,
Paving the way.

With these, Godzilla goes through the cities
Limping slightly.
The left one, which is a lover of peace
And fields of flowers,
And the right, which is a soldier, nothing more.

The Prodigal Son

—And I had become the destroyer of worlds
                              Oppenheimer

In an Alley off the Ginza, near the exclusive Twinning's tea house,
Godzilla waits patiently to be noticed by Dr. Oppenheimer,

Sitting by the window of the eighth floor rotunda. The curved glass
Of the building stretches the reflection of Godzilla's eye as he wavers

Back and forth, his mouth disappearing around
     the curve of the building
And down Ginza street. Children look up and recognize him,

They wave and are tugged by their parents who, not looking up
From beneath their own hands, do not see the giant lizard.

Dr. Oppenheimer has scheduled to meet his son for lunch
     at the exclusive
Tea house. Dr. Oppenheimer has never met his son
     before and so he

Wears a red tie and asks for a seat by the window. He orders
     a cup of Earl
Gray for 18 dollars U.S. Dr. Oppenheimer is the only foreigner

In the room, so he knows he will be recognized; already
     Japanese children
Are pointing and snickering and being shushed by their mothers.

While he waits Dr. Oppenheimer picks the white corners
     from the napkin
Beneath his tea cup, hunching over the white circle he has made

Around the dark liquid in the imported English China cup.
Dr. Oppenheimer stares down, thinking of the children
     he has made,

How their own special brightness is a quality he tried to
    instill in them,
Like tiger's teeth painted on the sides of P-39s or dragster cars.

Dr. Oppenheimer wonders if his children ever tinkered with cars
Or had the desire to drive fast and impress the girls.

Probably, he thinks, losing himself in the image of his eye floating,
Looking back at him through the dark liquid,

Unaware of the longing glance of Godzilla from the street below.

The Jesuit Cemetery on the Bluff

Tankers lie long like tea leaves in Tokyo Bay.
At the Jesuit Cemetery on the bluff
The stone crosses
Are marked in Roman letters,
Written, like crosses, with water.
Portuguese names reel under the Dragon's Tooth,
Used by masons
To mark forbidden stones. Here
White Christians hold hands
Beneath the mitered ground,
Headstones make promises
Of returns.
Jesuits at first came to know this view,
Eager to spread God, and for tea,
That soft green, presented in a round cup,
The rim girded, by design, with Dragon's scales,
As now Tokyo bay has a rim
Of concrete. Studies of the view
Are indissoluble, they grow nourished
On the rock-dressed bodies of foreigners only.
                    Therefore
Everything behind the boy
Who climbs a path through the stones
Disappears. His footsteps
Dress the hillside, patterns
On his sneaker soles
Cut swaths through stone
Like water.
Starlings in the trees break
With laughter as the sun
Glints across marble
And the names curiously
Darken to one another.
                    The names
Are everything
To no one.

The bay churns beneath the bluff,
Great waves slap at concrete, chewing at stone,
The Dragon's current, as if to say
There is a place where souls go home to,
But it is not here.

The Palace Moat

The black swans in the moat
Are linked by moonlight
And by water.

The emperor doesn't know of them.
The people see them as the emperor
Himself—black, aloof, untouchable.

What no one knows is that a boy
Will find a long black feather
On the dirty sidewalk

And press it into a book
As if it were mystery itself,
And forget it

For fifty years until, while
Cleaning his mother's house
After her death, he finds it

And realizes
That throughout his entire childhood
He had been unaware of himself.

But this is already too much.

Moss spreads
On the great stones
Of the palace walls.

Their great weight,
Their stillness.

Exile

Blather of urine soaked streets,
Straw along the way and rickshaw,
Pulled by a grandmother
Whose legs transcend themselves
In work, even as they carry her
Granddaughter.

The cock crows & its head is severed.
The headless cock is
A more divine medium than prayer.

The bricks along the temple wall transcend, also,
The street. They give nothing to
Nothing as a question asked
To the mountain.

Why? Why not.

This is the city of my exile.
The temple door with demons, beginning & ending,
An infinite snarl of tragedy
I get used to being lost in,
As the roads turn away
As the face of a woman turns
To transcend into candlelight.

I omit only the precipice of perception
Down a row of colored lights
Moving into darkness along the street.

I walk with character, the style of exile.
Only I, obscured by trees,
By the gallant shadow of my
Exiled person, with strong legs,
Strong shin bones and shank.

The rickshaw driver counters with laughter.

A foreigner is only so to himself
And the world.

Godface

How much do I have to prepare the mind
To know it sees destruction?

Can I just say the name?

If there are two ways of seeing god
Then there are two gods.

Within and without: meet me between
The sight and the seen.

Creator and destroyer: the eye
And thought that makes it real.

A sudden shiver, a slip.
There is no pain in curiosity,
Betray me to your curiosity.

I tremble to the way disaster
Is remembered.

Fingers coax my ruin from
The beach sands I have crumbled to.

Meet me with your godface,
We will agree each other's existence,

Even though truth empties
From the energy between the atoms:

Nucleus and electron,
Star and planet,

Face and the empty air around it
On fire with perception

And doubts perception. You are my
Tiny Machine.

Justification

In winter,
The physicists' feet
Are cold and wet.

Wearing the wrong shoes
They step into
Deep snow.

This is how the
Physicists are made to
Wonder about heat.

They praise the sun
For all that it makes them
Want of warmth.

But the cold eventually finds
The limitation of the toe,
And imaginable suns are born.

No one thinks of heat in August.
It is disregarded, hidden in
Its own pervasiveness.

Only the foot knows
The duration of snow. The half lives
Of half lives.

An amputated toe
Remembering heat
Is an isolated isotope.

Uranium Sky

Under Geiger test skies,
The choice we have left is whether to burn
Ourselves out as a cancer
Or to be our own oncologists,
Pointing the X-ray of god
And science at ourselves.

Radiation beats against our rooftops,
Pulses views into
Everywhere Technicolor.
The sound burns of morning
Though we don't know it
Because we have felt it all out lives.
It drags a melancholy from us
The same way our food is dragged
From the second pick-up window
At the McDonald's.
Order, then pay, then eat
Delirious flesh.
Radiation goes into our bodies
Like food, like fresh grain
Scattered for the chicken
Raised under the eternal
Fluorescent angel.
We are constantly pelted
By the sky until we are knocked out
Like a homerun nuclear test.

The sky crinkles its face
Like aluminum foil
Over a bowl of food.
Car antennas anticipate sunspots,
Crack military codes,
Slipping strike coordinates
Across the lips of Conway
Twitty, Johnny Cash and Elvis;

They triangulate and burn
The rich desert air with a
Razzle-dazzle-early-morning-lip-gloss
Shine, usually found
On snowy peaks like
The mangled sneer of a lynx
Lunging out from a glossy
High school football helmet.

We are blessed in the gestures of radiation
By its press-on nails which graze our
Fundamental need to clutch
At techno-industry
Like pigs in a pork truck
Lined up along the highway
During the hottest day of the year.
The sound of it is a ripping sound
Like pig tooth on pig flesh.

Incandescent Neurosis

I wouldn't put it in a pot
Though it could grow there
Like that hydroponic chicken
Listening to the hymns
Of fluorescent angels singing
Out in 60 ohms. No, it's not
Like that, though, it lingers
Beneath my ocean like
Mommy's wire hanger beatings.

It's not quite a flower
Either, though people have
Killed each other hunting
For orchids.
It's the feel of half rotted
Flesh and the fly
Drawing scent that drives
Me mad. Though it could
Just as easily have been
A formalized boredom.

Still, I can't put it away because
Then I'd be inefficient,
Left clinging to the neck
Of a wire hangar, a complete
Isolation to the boundaries
Of my highway world.

I get set off by the
Talk-show motor of my life,
Choking on diesel smoke
As the rumble of trucks
Drowns out my own voice
Telling me to kill
Anything that has
A shopping mall for a heart.

Godzilla Tries to Quit Smoking

Everything I have ever wanted has no legs.
It sits in restaurants and orders
Only the cheapest beers.
I wish it were as beautiful as the billboard
That can make children smoke.
Offering cigarettes to minors
Is the evolution of the lung:
A little jackpot of alveoli
Meshed with plant cells.

Wanting is a neurosis I prefer to ignore.
But it somehow manages to gurgle
Into my routine, driving a brand new
SUV, choking me with more diesel fumes,
Fracturing my civility.

Everything I have ever wanted proves
That gargling martinis should be part of my
Skill-set, it tells me that eating fast food
Is like dining on religion—
A big Buddha shake and a
Double Christ meal with cheese, please.

Like everything I have ever wanted
My little black alveoli want to come out
And sun themselves
In their own dark thongs.

News Report:

1.

Godzilla has not rampaged the fields.
Mostly he rages against the structures.
The city made of lines so softly yields,
As a house from space abstractly fractures.

The haiku masters, though concerned, are proud.
The wheat fields of America offer
An endless sky, like an ocean cloud.
Nebraska heaves under the weight of corn

The monster issues a communiqué:
His desire to make a U.S. visit,
"The land will be cleaned in one swipe," He says,
"I will submerge in wheat with the harvest."

Into land the ocean slowly scissors
No one swims there, it is too dangerous.

2.

Atop the cliffs, sighting posts
Left over from the war are
Alive again with eyes.

At night small lights
Outline the coast in
Rhinestone.

The monster wishes to visit Graceland.
Promises no damage if he can try on
A jumpsuit.

Great fins are spotted
On cars rising on long
Straight American highways.

3.

In a fit of grace
The haiku masters
Have committed suicide.

Eating their
Ink blocks one at a time
Until their mouths

Are black
With squid ink.
The last one

Threw himself off
A cliff.
Still clutching his brush.

4.

When his body washed up
A farmer found him
Rolling in the surf.

The brush hand
Rocked in the sand.
The farmer later admitted

That it was the most beautiful
Calligraphy he had
Ever seen.

But the ocean hiss
Wiped it clean
With a swipe of mist.

Godzilla's Birthday

The Baroness gave birth the minute history began to end.
The whole world seemed to sense the hour of delivery approaching.

It is said that people born out at sea may die three or four
    times at a dinner party.
The midwives were all men lost at war.

I remember moonlight and darkness said one. I can read,
    said another *but I can't*
Remember how to spell. What ever happened to the cannons?
    Asked the first.

They remind me of penises, said the Baroness in the pains of labor.
After the delivery, the midwives all lit cigarettes and passed
    them to the Baroness

And her baby. *I love the eyes,* said the baby,
Together we are born at sea.

Who Put the GOD in Godzilla

My skin is like a remote control
I can never find it when I need to.

Does this show how human I am?
Looking under the sofa for my scales,
Opening up the vacuum to check
The bag for my chest plates
Or that smooth transition from abdomen
To tail where some kind
Of genitals should be,
Finding only a mysterious zipper.

In the carpet depression my feet left,
I comb through the weave
With a quarter.
Each strand is a tiny vending machine
With a few mutating cells.

In my dreams I am a quarter
Dropped into the absolution box,
Small trails of saintly-ness stutter my vision,
A mottled piece of epidermis wedges into the box
And my vertical pupil is sliced into a cross.
I become biblical.

When I meet myself in the stairwell mirror,
The one that rises up between us,
We square to each other and I tell myself
I will save you from your rubbery self.

Godzilla Visits Camus in Hell

I only came back to get a beer
And ran into this hostility,
This suicidal wonder
Rolling his way into beer after beer
Instead of being crushed by that stone
As it rolls back over him.

He is trying to psyche me out,
Giving me the bar eye,
The gesture of argument, of war
Which passes through my cold blooded brain,
Into my cold fingers
And makes of them warring bodies…

It's a game of nerves. I feel the space between us
Until it is a friendly view of unfriendly places.

Suddenly, as if to confuse me, he grows wings,
And I remember I was an angel once too.
I smash a beer bottle on the bar.
I need a handful of broken glass
To turn on my brother.

Chrysanthemums

In the park beneath the cherry trees
A family is having a picnic,
The parents are watching their son
Play with a plastic Godzilla,
The roots of the cherry tree
Under the checked picnic cloth
Wither at a certain depth.

The cherry trees topple young.
And when they fall the park
Managers plant chrysanthemums
Within the hole exposed by withered roots.
The tree is cut up and burned
In the temple urn.

The parents don't care,
Don't wonder where their myths
Come from,
Don't worry about
Tigers hunting in Chinese mist,

Or how the face of the girl drowned
Beneath ice does not impress
The carp looking up from the
Underneath of nowhere.

Chrysanthemums turn their heads
Away from the ocean breeze.
The mother thinks she looks like them,
Wants to look like them, standing
Up to obscure something,
Letting the world forget its holes
And see instead flowers.

The wind dies down
Which doesn't mean anything.

The mother thinks
If she were round, like a hole in the ice,
Or a rising cloud, mushrooming
Back on herself, maybe
She could see

What she's done. Maybe she could see herself
As a child, standing with the multitude
At the Meiji Shrine, Harajuku,
Moving in for the new years blessing
With the other million believers.
She would give herself a hundred yen coin
To hurl over the heads of the crowd
And onto the protective apron
The priests spread around the steps like a bib.
Not as prayers for answers,
For money or for fame,
But only to see the real names of the stars
Behind, underneath.

She would throw the coin
She would give herself straight up
With the million other stars.